101 Celtic
BEASTS

101 Celtic
BEASTS

courtney davis

David and Charles

A DAVID & CHARLES BOOK
Copyright © David & Charles Limited 2007

David & Charles is an F+W Publications Inc. company
4700 East Galbraith Road
Cincinnati, OH 45236

First published in the UK in 2007

Text and illustrations copyright © Courtney Davis 2007

Courtney Davis has asserted his right to be identified
as author of this work in accordance with the Copyright,
Designs and Patents Act, 1988.

A catalogue record for this book is available from the
British Library.

ISBN-13: 978-0-7153-2432-5
ISBN-10: 0-7153-2432-2

Printed in Malaysia by KHL Printing Co Sdn Bhd
for David & Charles
Brunel House   Newton Abbot   Devon

Commissioning Editor   Neil Baber
Assistant Editor   Louise Clark
Designer   Eleanor Stafford
Production Controller   Kelly Smith

Visit our website at **www.davidandcharles.co.uk**

David & Charles books are available from all good bookshops;
alternatively you can contact our Orderline on 0870 9908222
or write to us at FREEPOST EX2 110, D&C Direct, Newton
Abbot, TQ12 4ZZ (no stamp required UK only); US customers
call 800-289-0963 and Canadian customers call 800-840-5220.

*This book is dedicated to the beasts that
inhabit the natural world and the unseen
worlds beyond.*

*Special thanks to Neil Baber for his valuable
input on the introduction and his help on the
rest of the 101 Celtic books.*

contents

introduction

Both literally and symbolically, animals were an important and integral part of the Celts' lives. These early people not only relied on animals for their survival but respected them, learned from them and honoured them. The different attributes of the beasts of land, sea and sky were closely studied, and particular creatures were associated with different powers and abilities. In Celtic stories, heroes, spirits and gods frequently 'shapeshift', or take on the form of an animal, in order to gain attributes such as wisdom or strength in battle.

The ancient Celts worshipped numerous deities, many of which took animal form, but generally they did not depict them in images, preferring abstract decoration. They perhaps considered it inappropriate to attempt to create images of gods. It was under Roman influence that images of Celtic deities began to appear, and animal images were used to decorate jewellery, weapons, monuments and, in the Christian period, manuscripts. Meanwhile, attempts were made by Julius Caesar and others to find parallels between the Roman gods and those of the Celts.

Celtic Totem Animals

Among the oldest and most revered of animals in the Celtic world was the bear. Though the brown bear was extinct in the British Isles by the 10th century, it survived in other parts of Europe. The bear's ability to sleep through the winter months, effecting a sort of rebirth in the spring, made it a powerful emblem of regeneration. Its symbolic role was shared by the serpent, which was also an important creature to the Celts and, like the bear, a major religious symbol long before they emerged as a distinct people. In addition to hibernation, the serpent's periodic emergence from its own shed skin led people to believe that it had the power of self-renewal. It was thus a symbol of life, fertility, rejuvenation, regeneration and immortality. When depicted coiled with its tail in its mouth, the serpent also symbolized infinity and omnipotence.

The Celts believed that the deer was the oldest of all creatures and associated it with Cernunnos, the horned god of nature and hunting. Deer seem to have played an important role in Celtic culture, appearing often in both pre-Christian mythology and the lives of the saints, thanks no doubt to their qualities of speed, elegance and beauty and their keen senses. White stags were considered to be creatures of the otherworld, and in Celtic myths their appearance heralded some profound change in the lives of the protagonists.

The veneration of cows and bulls also has a long history in Europe. Among the beasts depicted in the famous cave paintings at Lascaux in France, made at some time between 17,000 and 12,000 BC, were several cows and the five huge bulls that gave rise to the naming of one chamber as the 'Hall of Bulls'. The cow was a symbol of the sanctity of motherhood; milk sustained the life force and drinking milk from a sacred cow was seen as a way of communing with divinity. It was also believed to heal wounds sustained in battle, and a mother's milk was said to have curative powers.

Strong, fast, magnificent and above all useful, the horse was essential to the Celtic lifestyle, as it was to prove for succeeding cultures for many centuries. Representative of the sovereignty goddess Epona, the 'Great Mare', the horse was particularly revered by warriors, to whom she gave protection. Throughout northern Europe a horse sacrifice was considered an essential part of the funeral rites for a dead warrior. Such rituals continued to be performed up to the 10th century AD in Norway, despite attempts by the recently Christianized kings to stop the practice. There is evidence that similar rites persisted in England until the 15th century, when it was still the custom to bleed horses for luck on St Stephen's Day, the day after Christmas.

The salmon probably appears in Celtic iconography more often than any other animal, and symbolically it is always associated with wisdom and the acquisition of knowledge. Since this symbolism was already well established, the fish was readily adopted by Celtic Christians as a symbol of Christianity. It had been associated with the religion since its earliest times, because the Greek word for fish, *ichthus*, could be read as an acrostic consisting of the initial letters of the words *Iesous Christos Theou Yios Soter* ('Jesus Christ, Son of God, Saviour').

Boars and pigs were associated with fertility, wealth and abundance, probably because the pig fattens and multiplies at a prolific rate. Its speedy growth and fertility led to its use as a totem to ensure a good harvest: ancient pig figurines have been found bearing signs of impressed grain, while some vegetation goddesses were portrayed wearing pig masks.

Dogs or hounds are common symbols of loyalty and fidelity. Cats appear only occasionally in Celtic myths, but can be found on the pages of many illuminated manuscripts, possibly because they made good pets and useful pest controllers around the monasteries. The intricate decoration on the *Chi Rho* page of the Book of Kells includes tiny images of cats and mice playing together. There is little evidence that larger cats had much place in the Celtic world, but the facts that the symbol of St Mark the Evangelist was a lion and that lions featured in bible stories such as that of Daniel would have given the monks ample opportunities to depict the magnificent animals.

Many birds, particularly eagles, ravens, hawks, falcons, cranes and swans, appear in Celtic designs. Birds usually represented prophetic knowledge and were particularly associated with war and the battlefield. They were thought to be omens, which if properly interpreted might provide information about future events. The raven was particularly associated with death and the battlefield, whereas the eagle, regarded as the greatest of all birds by many cultures, was revered for its ability to soar, apparently into the sun, making it an ideal spirit guide to the 'upperworld' and also a symbol of solar divinity. Eagles appear frequently on Celtic cult objects and coins. The crane, now extinct in Britain, was an important bird in the Celtic tradition. Cranes were the guardians of the 'otherworld' and several myths involve heroes or gods being transformed into these birds. Likewise a number of Irish tales involve transformation into a swan.

Manuscript Illumination and the Evangelists' Symbols

Celtic tales, laws and history had always been passed down in oral tradition, but with the Christian monks came the beginning of the production of books. However, for early Celtic writers brought up in the bardic tradition, it would not have been enough to copy the plain text. In the retelling of tales it was the custom of the bards to embellish their material with expression and elaboration, even with sound effects and music. This helped them to engage their audience, drawing them deeply into the tale. Naturally the scribes were predisposed to reproduce these meanderings in their copying of manuscripts by adding ever more elaborate decoration, as Celtic craftsmen had always done in the adornment of tools, weapons, monuments and artifacts of every kind. Christianity had always made use of symbolism, especially as a means of teaching people who could not read. By established tradition, certain beasts came to be associated with Christ, the Virgin Mary and the saints in Christian iconography. A fish or a lamb was most commonly used to represent Christ, while a dove stood for the Holy Spirit. The most frequently reproduced symbols by far were those of the four evangelists: a man for Matthew, a lion for Mark, a bull for Luke, and an eagle for John. In the Bible, these four creatures first appear together in the opening chapter of the Book of Ezekiel, which describes a vision of God:

Also out of the midst thereof came the likeness of four living creatures. And this was their appearance; they had the likeness of a man.
And every one had four faces, and every one had four wings.
And their feet were straight feet; and the sole of their feet was like the sole of a calf's foot: and they sparkled like the colour of burnished brass.
And they had the hands of a man under their wings on their four sides; and they four had their faces and their wings.
Their wings were joined one to another; they turned not when they went; they went every one straight forward.
As for the likeness of their faces, they four had the face of a man, and the face of a lion, on the right side: and they four had the face of an ox on the left side; they four also had the face of an eagle.

If these faces were to be understood as aspects of God, and their function was to proclaim God's greatness, then it followed that they would be appropriate symbols for the four gospels, which were so central to the Christian message.

The bull and the eagle in particular were beasts already beloved of the Celts. The four symbols of the evangelists found particular favour with the gospel illuminators, but they are also commonly found in the decorated stone and metalwork of the Christian era.

Beasts in Celtic Design

The fluid and inventive patterning of Celtic art has great movement and vitality, and while this can already be seen in early spiral or knotwork designs, the animals woven into the patterns add the vitality and dynamism of living creatures. When the animals come charged with symbolic meaning, Celtic beast designs become even more powerful and compelling.

The ancient traditions and beliefs of the Celtic people, together with the symbolism of the Christian era, are the sources for the wide variety of beasts found in Celtic art: living creatures transformed into powerful symbolic representations by distinctive Celtic designs. In this book I have created designs based on many of the great works of Celtic art. In the first chapter they are taken from stone crosses, slabs and other monuments, and in the second chapter from a wide range of metal artifacts. The third chapter celebrates the illuminated gospel books that represent the pinnacle of achievement in Anglo-Saxon art. The final chapter presents my modern interpretations of Celtic designs, using the great tradition and practice of an ancient art to create contemporary styles.

designs
in stone

designs in stone

Serpent carved on a 6th-century symbol stone. The symbolism of the accompanying Z-shaped rod design is uncertain. *Newton, Aberdeenshire, Scotland*

designs in stone

This symbol on the 9th-century carved stone at Meigle is often referred to as an 'elephant' by historians; other versions can be found on early stone monuments in Scotland.
Meigle, Perth and Kinross, Scotland

Fine portrayal of a stag from the Eassie stone, a 9th-century cross slab.
Eassie, Angus, Scotland

Lion, symbol of St Mark the Evangelist, decorating an 8th-century cross slab.
Papil, Shetland, Scotland

Entwined sea horses from one of the early 9th-century cross slabs in Aberlemno churchyard. *Aberlemno, Angus, Scotland*

designs in stone

An eagle carved on a 7th-century incised slab. *Birdsay, Orkney, Scotland*

Powerful image of a wolf, a beast regarded as a useful guide to and from the underworld, from a 7th-century stone carving. *Inverness Museum and Art Gallery, Scotland*

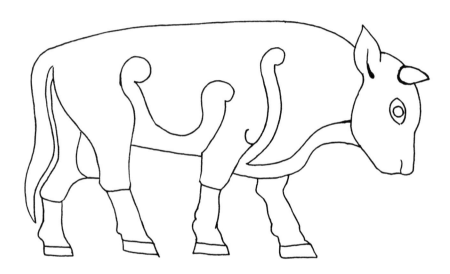

Bull from a 7th-century stone carving. There are other virtually identical versions of this design in the Royal Museum, Edinburgh, and the British Museum, London. *Elgin Museum, Scotland*

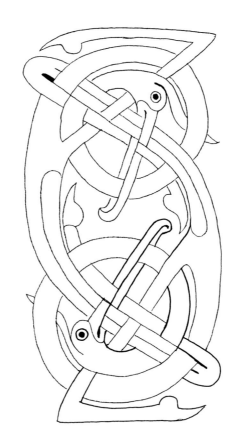

Detail of two interwoven beasts with elongated snouts or beaks from a 9th-century cross slab. *Aberlemno, Angus, Scotland*

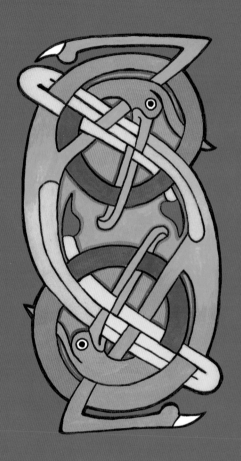

Boar adapted from a design carved on a sandstone pillar statue of the 1st century BC. *Euffigneix, Haute-Marne, France.*

designs in stone

Entwined beasts from a 7th-century rectangular plaque. This zoomorphic pattern is
similar to decoration on artifacts from the Sutton Hoo hoard and in the Book of Durrow.
Southampton City Museum, England

Crouched lion with a serpent tongue, adapted from a detail of a 12th-century stone carving over an arch. *Tuam, Galway, Ireland*

Design of a dog biting the head of a serpent adapted from a low-relief carving on the early 8th-century Aberlemno cross slab. *Aberlemno, Angus, Scotland*

Celtic and Viking art began to merge after the Viking invasions of Britain and Ireland. This design of the Scandinavian 'great beast' with a serpent appears on an 11th-century Viking tomb found in St Paul's Cathedral churchyard. *Guildhall Museum, London*

designs in metalwork

Entwined beast from the 12th-century shrine of St Lachtin, showing the strong influence of Viking Urnes style in the work of Irish craftsmen of this period.
National Museum of Ireland, Dublin

designs in metalwork

Dragon adapted from the Gundestrup cauldron of the 1st century BC, a silver vessel decorated with Celtic deities and numerous animals, both real and mythological. *Nationalmuseet, Copenhagen*

Bull-headed silver torc (neck ring) of the 2nd century BC from Trichtingen. It may have been worn as a sign of status and may have links with the god Cernunnos, who is always depicted wearing such a torc. *Würtembergisches Landesmuseum, Stuttgart, Germany*

Detail from a gold coin of the 3rd–1st centuries BC. showing a mare suckling a foal.
Bibliothéque Nationale, Paris

Detail from a gold coin of the 2nd–1st centuries BC showing a huge wolf turning its face towards the sun and moon. *Bibliothéque Nationale, Paris*

designs in metalwork

Human-headed horse from the lid of a bronze wine flagon of the 5th–4th centuries BC, reflecting the prominence of shapeshifting in stories of Celtic heroes.
Museum für Vor- und Frühgeschichte, Saarbrücken, Germany

designs in metalwork

Winged horse. a mythological beast common to many cultures. from the terminal of a gold torc. or neck ring. of the 5th century BC. *Vix, Côte d'Or, France*

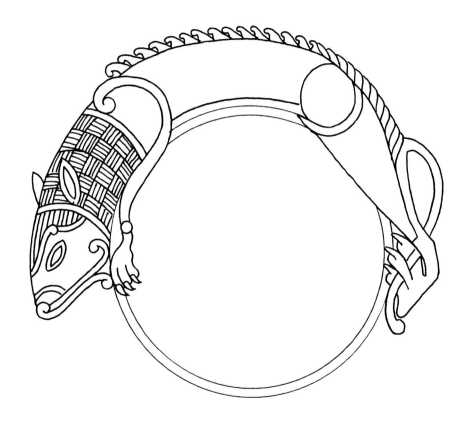

Beast forming the handle of a bronze wine flagon of the 5th–4th centuries BC.
Vorgeschichtliches Museum, Friedrich-Schiller-Universität, Jena, Germany

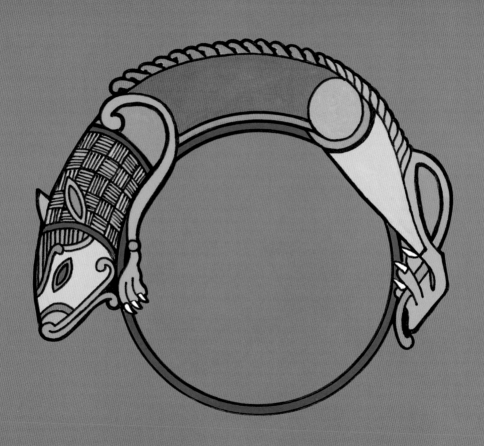

designs in metalwork

twenty-three

Enamelled bronze dragonesque brooch dating from the 1st century AD.
British Museum, London

twenty-four

Early bronze belt hook from the 4th century BC. *Hölzelsau, Kufstein, Austria*

Adapted interpretation of a lion from a 9th-century cast silver annular brooch.
National Museum of Ireland, Dublin

Design from a copper alloy horse harness mount from the 9th century, of Irish origin but in a style showing Viking influence. *Universitetets Oldsaksamling, Oslo*

One of two filigree beasts decorating an 8th-century brooch pin.
National Museum of Scotland, Edinburgh

designs in metalwork

Eagle, the symbol of St John the Evangelist, in a design from the early 11th-century Soiscél Molaise, or book shrine of St Molaise. *National Museum of Ireland, Dublin*

Lion, symbol of St Mark the Evangelist and one of the motifs on the Soiscél Molaise book shrine. *National Museum of Ireland, Dublin*

Bull, symbol of St Luke the Evangelist, in a design from the Soiscél Molaise book shrine.
National Museum of Ireland, Dublin

thirty-one

Entwined serpents from the Hunterston brooch, one of the earliest surviving penannualar brooches, dating from the late 7th century. *National Museum of Scotland, Edinburgh*

Celtic beast originally created in silver and gold filigree on the Hunterston brooch.
National Museum of Scotland, Edinburgh

Design from the Hunterston brooch. *National Museum of Scotland, Edinburgh*

Detail from the Cross of Cong, an elaborate processional cross of oak covered in gilt-bronze, made for King Turlach O'Connor in 1123. *National Museum of Ireland, Dublin*

Motif from the filigree decoration on the early 12th-century Cross of Cong, which was made to house a relic of the True Cross. *National Museum of Ireland, Dublin*

Design based on the Viking-influenced decoration on the 11th-century Lismore crozier.
The beasts are similar to designs in the earlier Book of Durrow.
National Museum of Ireland, Dublin

designs in metalwork

Viking Urnes-style beasts decorating the 11th-century shrine of St Patrick's bell.
National Museum of Ireland, Dublin

Entwined beasts from the intricate gold filigree decoration on the 11th-century shrine of St Patrick's bell. *National Museum of Ireland, Dublin*

Design from a section of an 8th-century silver bowl from the St Ninian's Isle hoard.
Royal Museum, Edinburgh

Filigree pattern of a beast from the Tara brooch, made in the 8th century, considered the golden age of Celtic craftsmanship in metalwork. *National Museum of Ireland, Dublin*

forty-one

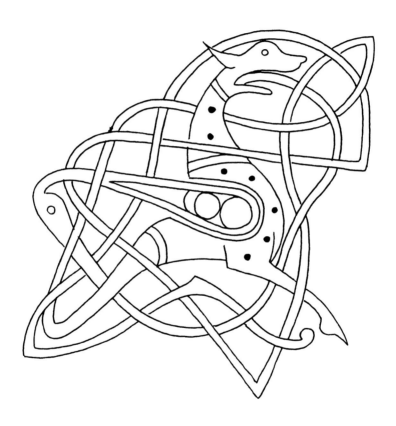

Chip-carved design from a silver-gilt linked pin of the 8th–9th centuries.
British Museum, London

Design of intertwined beasts on a silver-gilt pin from the 8th–9th-century Pentney hoard, found in Norfolk, England. *British Museum, London*

Fine beast design from a silver-gilt pin from the Pentney hoard. *British Museum, London*

Forty-Four

Entwined beasts from a 7th-century gold buckle with niello inlay from the Sutton Hoo ship burial. The beasts are similar to a procession of long-snouted animals in a border in the Book of Durrow. *British Museum, London*

Speckled beast on an 8th-century silver-gilt finger ring.
Victoria and Albert Museum, London

Interlocked birds on a early 9th-century silver pin. *Brandon Remembrance Playing Field Committee, Bury St Edmunds, Suffolk, England*

Early 9th-century design in niello inlay consisting of a half-length zoo-anthropomorphic representation of St John. *British Museum, London*

designs in illuminated manuscripts

forty-eight

Interlaced beasts from the late 7th-century Book of Durrow, similar to those decorating artifacts found in the Sutton Hoo ship burial. *Trinity College, Dublin*

forty-nine

Adapted from a border in the 7th century Book of Durrow. *Trinity College, Dublin*

Design based on a panel from the late seventh century Book of Durrow, which is the earliest surviving fully, illuminated Gospel book. *Trinity College, Dublin*

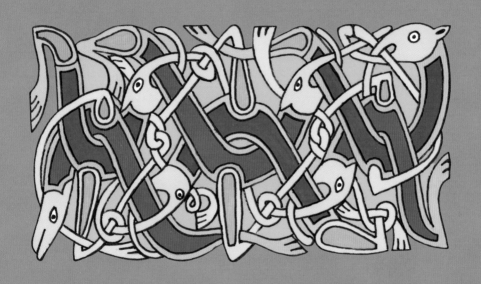

fifty~one

Entwined hounds in a detail from the 7th-century Durham Gospels.
Durham Cathedral Library, England

Three entwined bird heads from the Durham Gospels. Three was a sacred number for the pagan Celts and designs with a triple aspect were adopted by the Celtic monks to symbolize the Holy Trinity. *Durham Cathedral Library, England*

Section of a border adapted from the Durham Gospels.
Durham Cathedral Library, England

It is thought that the birds portrayed in the late 7th-century Lindisfarne Gospels may be cormorants, part of the rich wildlife of the island of Lindisfarne. *British Library, London*

fifty~five

Dogs from the Lindisfarne Gospels. In Christian symbology the dog, functioning as a
sheepdog, represented the priest guiding his flock. *British Library, London*

Entwined hound design from the Lindisfarne Gospels. The hound, primarily a hunting animal, was the favourite beast of the monks for gracing the pages of illuminated manuscripts. *British Library, London*

fifty-seven

Modified border from the Lindisfarne Gospels. All winged beings were used to symbolize spirituality. *British Library, London*

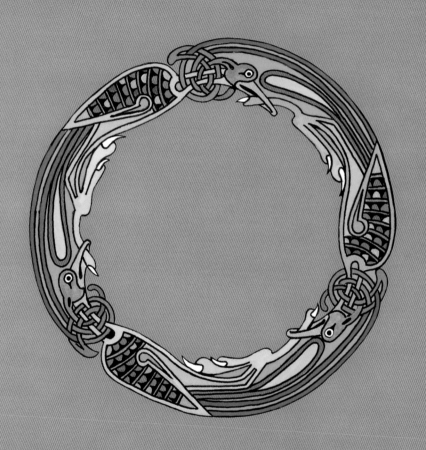

Pattern of entwined hounds from the Lindisfarne Gospels. *British Library, London*

fifty~nine

Birds and hounds entwined from the Lindisfarne Gospels. *British Library, London*

Bird heads from a terminal at the end of an initial in the Lindisfarne Gospels.
British Library, London

Entwined birds from the mid-8th-century Gospel of St Chad.
Lichfield Cathedral Chapter Library, Staffordshire, England

Border of birds adapted from the mid-8th-century Gospel of St Chad.
Lichfield Cathedral Chapter Library, Staffordshire, England

A bird entangled with two serpents from the 8th-century Leningrad Gospels.
Russian National Library, St Petersburg

designs in illuminated manuscripts

Motif from St Matthew's Gospel in the Leningrad Gospels. Because of many similarities with the Lichfield Gospels, it is believed that this book was produced at the same time and in the same monastery. *Russian National Library, St Petersburg*

sixty-five

Detail from the Leningrad Gospels. *Russian National Library, St Petersburg*

A figure, possibly a deer, from the Leningrad Gospels.
Russian National Library, St Petersburg

sixty–seven

The eagle, symbol of St John the Evangelist, from the 9th-century Macdurnan Gospels.
Lambeth Palace Library, London

sixty–eight

The calf, symbol of St Luke the Evangelist, from the 9th-century Macdurnan Gospels.
Lambeth Palace Library, London

Entwined dogs from the Durham Cassiodorus, an 8th-century illuminated copy of his exposition of the Psalms. *Durham Cathedral Library, England*

Detail of a dog surrounded by heavy knotwork from the 8th-century Durham Cassiodorus.
Durham Cathedral Library, England

Possibly a horse or deer-like animal from the Gospel of St Gatien, produced in Brittany in the late 8th or early 9th century. *Bibliothèque Nationale, Paris*

Possibly a horse or deer-like animal from the Gospel of St Gatien, produced in Brittany in the late 8th or early 9th century. *Bibliothèque Nationale, Paris*

seventy–three

Section from a large illuminated initial in the early 9th-century Book of Armagh.
Trinity College, Dublin

Entwined birds in a detail from the Corpus Christi Gospel Fragment, an early 9th-century manuscript. *Corpus Christi College, Cambridge, England*

seventy-five

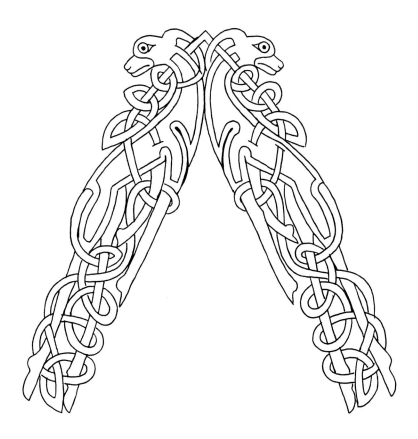

Design adapted from a section of the Incarnation initial from the 8th-century Stockholm Codex Aureus. An inscription on one of the pages tells of the book's return after a Viking raid in exchange for a payment of gold. *Kungliga Biblioteket, Stockholm*

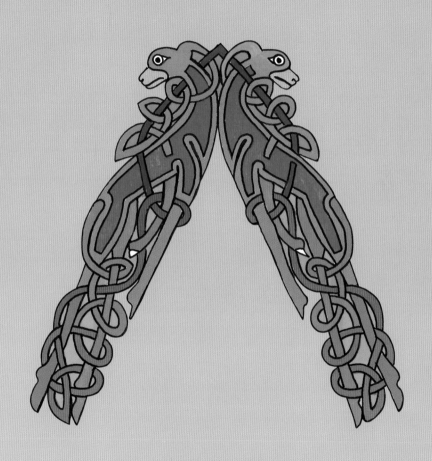

Modified image of a stag from the 8th-century Vespasian Psalter. *British Library, London*

Interlaced serpents from the 9th-century Book of Kells. *Trinity College, Dublin*

Design adapted from the Book of Kells. depicting an eagle clutching a salmon in its talons.
Trinity College, Dublin

seventy–nine

Detail of a cat with a mouse on its back from the Book of Kells. *Trinity College, Dublin*

Detail of a hare. an animal associated with the moon in Celtic mythology. adapted from a page of the Book of Kells. *Trinity College, Dublin*

In the symbology of this initial from the Book of Kells the peacock may depict Christ, and the hands around its throat may be those of the Pharisees, attempting to ensnare him. *Trinity College, Dublin*

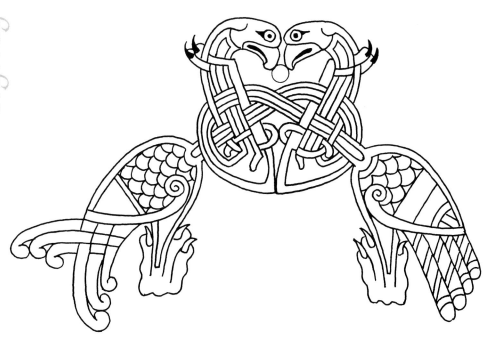

Peacocks from the Book of Kells. It was believed that the peacock's flesh was so hard it would not putrefy, so it symbolized the incorruptibility of Christ. *Trinity College, Dublin*

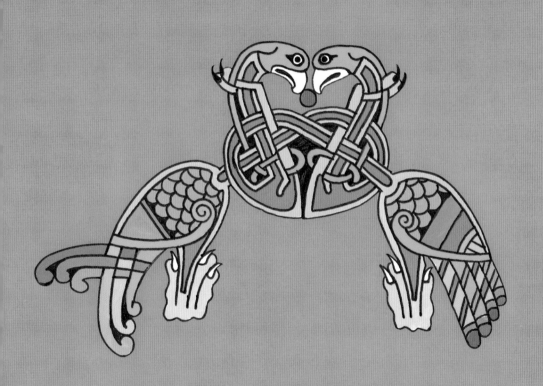

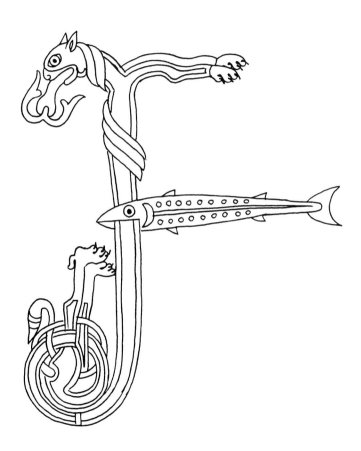

Initial from the Book of Kells formed from two Christian symbols: the fish (representing Christ and the soul) and the lion (resurrection). *Trinity College, Dublin*

Design of knotted snakes from the Book of Kells. *Trinity College, Dublin*

Section of a border from the Book of Kells. *Trinity College, Dublin*

Horseman from the Book of Kells. *Trinity College, Dublin*

Initial from the 11th-century Liber Hymnorum. Instead of intricate knotwork, foliage and tendrils are used in the style of Scandinavian Ringerike art, illustrating the demise of the earlier style of gospel illumination. *Trinity College, Dublin*

Intertwined beast initial from the late 11th-century Psalter of Ricemarcus.
Trinity College, Dublin

Initial from the Book of Glendalough, a 12th-century Irish manuscript.
Bodleian Library, Oxford

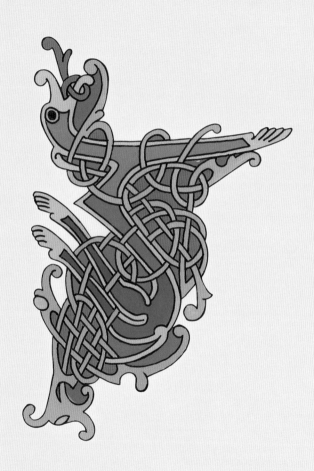

modern
designs

Peacocks signified the incorruptibility of Christ in Celtic art; these entwined birds are in the style of the Lindisfarne Gospels.

The cow symbolized the sacredness of motherhood. Drinking milk from a sacred cow was an early form of communion with divinity and was believed to heal battle wounds.

The lion, the symbol of St Mark the Evangelist, in the style of the Book of Kells.

The great 6th-century Welsh bard Taliesin claimed to have spent time in the form of a buck. a speckled cat and a goat during his life.

The unicorn is a mythical animal symbolizing chastity and purity. Its single horn, signifying unity, purifies whatever it touches.

Birds symbolize the soul or spirit. The knotwork in this design represents the binding of the soul in the physical world, from which it seeks to be released.

Entwined birds.

The salmon is a boundary crosser, living in the sea but returning to a freshwater river to mate; in crossing from salt water to fresh it was believed to bring about transformation.

Deer with knotwork. A story of St Patrick tells that when he was on the run from King Leoghaire, who wished to do him harm, he blessed his eight companions and they changed into a group of eight deer and escaped into the woods.

modern designs

Entwined hounds. The hound was the totem animal of the pre-eminent Ulster hero
Cuchulainn and a Celtic symbol of steadfastness and loyalty.

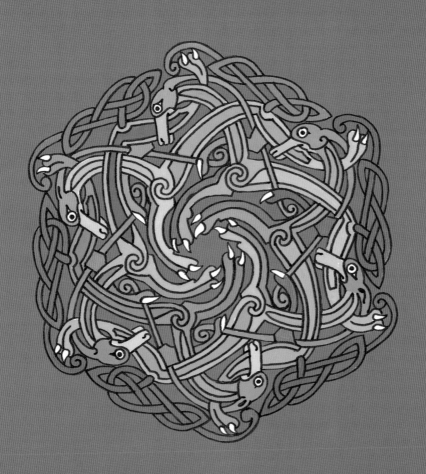

Swans have beneficent associations in Celtic lore. Their skin and feathers were used to make the bard's ceremonial cloak, aligning his poetry with the language of the birds.

one hundred and one

Cernunnos the horned god is traditionally depicted seated, surrounded by animals over which he is particularly powerful, among them the stag and the boar. In his left hand, he holds a ram-headed serpent and in his right a torc. He also wears a torc around his throat.

Books by Courtney Davis

The Celtic Saints,
Blandford Press, 1995

The Celtic Image,
Blandford Press, 1996

Celtic Ornament: The Art of the Scribe,
Blandford Press, 1996

Celtic Initials and Alphabets,
Blandford Press, 1997

Celtic Illumination: The Irish School,
Thames & Hudson, 1998

Celtic Tattoo: Workbook One,
Awen Press, 2002

Celtic Tattoo: Workbook Two,
Awen Press, 2003

Viking Tattoo: Workbook,
Awen Press, 2003

More information and examples of the art of Courtney Davis
can be found at: **www.celtic-art.com**

Bibliography

Symbolism of the Celtic Cross,
Derek Bryce, Llanerch Enterprises, 1989

Celtic Design: A Sourcebook of Patterns and Motifs,
Iain Zaczek, Studio Editions, 1995

Celtic Art: The Methods of Construction,
George Bain, Constable, 1951

Celtic Art in Pagan and Christian Times,
J. Romilly Allen, Bracken Books, 1993

The Lindisfarne Gospels,
Janet Backhouse, Phaidon Press, 1981

The Book of Kells,
Bernard Meehan, Thames & Hudson, 1994

The Book of Kells,
Peter Brown, Thames & Hudson, 1980

Celtic and Anglo-Saxon Painting,
Carl Nordenfalk, Chatto and Windus, 1977

Anglo-Saxon Art,
David M. Wilson, Thames and Hudson, 1984

From Durrow to Kells,
George Henderson, Thames and Hudson, 1987